Wyatt Earp & Doc Holliday: The West's Greatest Gunslingers

By Charles River Editors

About Charles River Editors

Charles River Editors was founded by Harvard and MIT alumni to provide superior editing and original writing services, with the expertise to create digital content for publishers across a vast range of subject matter. In addition to providing original digital content for third party publishers, Charles River Editors republishes civilization's greatest literary works, bringing them to a new generation via ebooks. Signup to receive updates about new books as we publish them, and visit charlesrivereditors.com for more information.

Introduction

Wyatt Earp (1848-1929)

"For my handling of the situation at Tombstone, I have no regrets. Were it to be done over again, I would do exactly as I did at that time. If the outlaws and their friends and allies imagined that they could intimidate or exterminate the Earps by a process of assassination, and then hide behind alibis and the technicalities of the law, they simply missed their guess." – Wyatt Earp

Of all the colorful characters that inhabited the West during the 19th century, the most famous of them all is Wyatt Earp (1848-1929), who has long been regarded as the embodiment of the Wild West. Considered the "toughest and deadliest gunman of his day", Earp symbolized the swagger, the heroism, and even the lawlessness of the West, notorious for being a law enforcer, gambler, saloon keeper, and vigilante. The Western icon is best known for being a sheriff in Tombstone, but before that he had been arrested and jailed several times himself, in one case escaping from prison, and he was not above gambling and spending time in "houses of ill-fame".

The seminal moment in Earp's life also happened to be the West's most famous gunfight, the Gunfight at the O.K. Corral, which famously pitted Earp, his brothers Morgan and Virgil, and Doc Holliday against Billy Clanton, Tom McLaury and Frank McLaury. Though the gunfight lasted less than a minute, it is still widely remembered as the climactic event of the period, representing lawlessness and justice, vendettas, and a uniquely Western moral code. For Earp, the aftermath led to assassination attempts on his brothers, one of which was successful, touching off the "Earp Vendetta Ride".

By the end of the 19th century, Earp was already a poignant symbol of that time and day, having permanently etched his name in the folklore of the West, but he stayed out west, engaging in everything from gold mining to vigilante justice on the Mexican border. A living legend, he even served as an advisor to early Hollywood, which was already pumping out Western movies. When he died in 1929 at the age of 80, one of the West's toughest fighers and one of its longest survivors had finally passed

Wyatt Earp & Doc Holliday details Earp's amazing life and career, including all of its famous ups and infamous downs, while also analyzing his legacy and the mythology that has enveloped his story. Along with pictures of important people, places, and events in his life, you will learn about Wyatt Earp like you never have before, in no time at all.

John Henry "Doc" Holliday (1851-1887)

"Doc was a dentist, not a lawman or an assassin, whom necessity had made a gambler; a gentleman whom disease had made a frontier vagabond; a philosopher whom life had made a caustic wit; a long lean ash-blond fellow nearly dead with consumption, and at the same time the most skillful gambler and the nerviest, speediest, deadliest man with a six-gun that I ever knew."
– Wyatt Earp

Of all the colorful characters that inhabited the West during the 19th century, the man who has earned an enduring legacy as the region's quirkiest is John Henry "Doc" Holliday (1851-1887), a dentist turned professional gambler who was widely recognized as one of the fastest draws in the West. In fact, the only thing that might have been faster than the deadly gunman's draw was his violent temper, which was easily set off when Holliday was drunk. By the early 1880s, Holliday had been arrested nearly 20 times.

That said, there were plenty of men in the West who gambled, drank, and dueled, and Holliday may have been lumped in with those whose names were forgotten but for his association with Wyatt Earp. It was this friendship that led to Holliday's role in the West's most famous shootout, the Gunfight at the O.K. Corrall, as well as the Earp Vendetta Ride. For those two events alone, Holliday's legacy has endured, and his unique characteristics have added a mystique, legendary quality to it.

Next to Earp, Holliday might be the second most recognizable name among the legends of the West, and yet several details of his life remain sketchy. *Wyatt Earp & Doc Holliday* chronicles Holliday's life, while also analyzing his legacy and the mythology that has enveloped his story. Along with pictures of important people, places, and events in his life, you will learn about Doc Holliday like you never have before, in no time at all.

A photo believed to be of Doc Holliday in Tombstone in the early 1880s

Bat Masterson and Wyatt Earp (right) in Dodge City, 1876.

Wyatt Earp & Doc Holliday: The West's Greatest Gunslingers
About Charles River Editors
Introduction
   Chapter 1: Wyatt's Early Years
      Childhood Years
      Return to His Family
   Chapter 2: Doc's Early Years
      John Henry Holliday, D.D.S.
   Chapter 3: Wyatt Earp, Law Enforcer
   Chapter 4: Wyatt Earp and Doc Holliday Head West
      Earp's Path to Tombstone
      Doc Heads to Texas
      Wyatt and Doc's Friendship
      Doc Heads to Las Vegas, New Mexico
   Chapter 5: Becoming Legends in Arizona
      Wyatt Strikes Out
      Doc Heads to Tombstone
      The Oriental Saloon

    Wyatt's Early Law Enforcement Career in Tombstone
    The Origins of the Feud with the Clantons and McLaurys
    The Gunfight at the O.K. Corral
    The Earps Become Targets
    The Earp Vendetta Ride
Chapter 6: Doc Holliday's Final Years
Chapter 7: Wyatt and Sadie Roam the West
    San Diego
    San Francisco
    Alaska, Seattle, and Back Again
    Alaska and Nevada
    Los Angeles
    Hollywood
    The Quest to Set the Record Straight
Chapter 8: Wyatt Dies but a Star is Born
Chapter 9: The Doc Holliday Legend
Wyatt Earp Bibliography
Doc Holliday Bibliography

Chapter 1: Wyatt's Early Years

Childhood Years

Wyatt and his mother

Nicholas Porter Earp was a wanderer. As a young man, he led his family as they crisscrossed the Plains and into the western United States, always in search of the next "big thing" that could put money in his pocket. On July 27, 1840, the widower with one son married Virginia Ann Cooksey in Hartford, Kentucky. They had eight children, including Nick Earp's fourth son, Wyatt Berry Stapp Earp. Wyatt was born on March 19, 1848 in Monmouth, Illinois, and was named for his father's captain in the Mexican-American War. Shortly after he was born, Nick moved the family to a farm in Pella, Iowa, where the family would remain for several years.

Wyatt's boyhood home in Pella

Being the son of Nick Earp could be challenging. He was known to drink to excess, didn't always pay his bills, and could be a bully. His sons were a close-knit group, to the point that Wyatt tried to run away and join his older brothers, Newton, James, and Virgil, when they were fighting for the Union in the Civil War. More than once, Nick found 13 year-old Wyatt and had to bring him back home. Wyatt became a proficient - if unwilling - farmer by the time the Earps pulled up stakes again in 1864, this time to join a wagon train headed to California.

It was in California that the Earps heard the news that Robert E. Lee's Confederate Army of Northern Virginia had surrendered to Ulysses S. Grant and the Army of the Potomac at Appomattox, informally bringing the Civil War to an end. With the end of the war came the true unification of the United States, at least in geography if not in ideals and culture. Considered by many to be the greatest engineering innovation of the 19th century, the Transcontinental Railroad would not only bring people, industry, goods, and ideas west, it would provide Wyatt with work as a young man and expose him to the type of rough and tumble environment that he revisited time and again throughout his life.

Nothing made the Wild West wild more than the railroad. As the Union Pacific forged its way west from Omaha, temporary towns referred to as "Hell on Wheels" popped up in anticipation of the railroad workers. These men worked hard during the day, often in extreme conditions in remote locations. They needed somewhere to spend their money and looked forward to the chance to blow off some steam. Card players, drinkers, prostitutes, and thieves were as much a part of the railroad worker's life as laying track, and young Wyatt saw it all as he graded track for the rail line. His time spent working for the Union Pacific in Wyoming in 1868 taught him two skills that soon became part of the Wyatt Earp legend: boxing and gambling.

19 year old Wyatt

Return to His Family

By 1869, Earp had migrated back across the country and rejoined his family in Lamar, Missouri. Still only 21 years old, he had already lived a nomadic life and now appeared to be settling down. As a young adult, he replaced his father as the town constable when Nick became justice of the peace, and it was Nick who performed the ceremony when Wyatt married Urilla Sutherland, the daughter of a local hotel owner, his father performs the ceremony. With his new wife, Wyatt bought a house on the outskirts of town, and it wasn't long before Urilla was pregnant. With a job, a wife, a house, and a child on the way, Earp's life seemed to be a picture of stability.

The tranquil life of Wyatt Earp lasted less than a year. Within a year, 21 year-old Urilla and her unborn child were dead, for reasons that are still not completely clear. Some later accounts blamed typhoid or complications related to childbirth, but whatever the actual cause of her death, Urilla's brothers blamed Wyatt for their sister's death, leading to a brawl in the streets of Lamar between the Earp brothers and the Sutherland brothers.

Shortly after that incident, with his unsettled life seemingly in shambles, Wyatt sold the house that he had purchased just a few months earlier and left Lamar a changed man.

Chapter 2: Doc's Early Years

When John Henry Holliday was born on August 14, 1851, in Spalding County, Georgia, the Southern Frontier was less than two decades removed from being the land of the Cherokees. His father, Henry Burroughs Holliday, was a self-made man who believed in the Southern codes of honor, independence, and community. As a reward for assisting the First Georgia volunteers in removing the Cherokees and starting them on their Trail of Tears west, Henry Holliday was given 160 acres of land in Pike County.

Henry settled in the town of Griffin, which would later be part of the newly created Spalding County. For a man seeking a life of respectability, he could have not chosen a better wife than Alice Jane McKey of the South Carolina McKeys. Beautiful, fair-haired, and a lover of music, Alice became Henry's wife on January 8, 1849, three months before her 20th birthday. By the time Alice and Henry were expecting their first child, Henry was a respected man in the community, working as a druggist and accumulating land on the side. Martha Eleanora was born on December 3, 1849, but the baby was frail from the start and died half a year later on June 12, 1850.

When John Henry was born a little over a year later, Henry and Alice's grief turned to joy. Not even his cleft palate, which was surgically repaired in a delicate procedure for the times, could dampen their spirits. Their first-born son was a symbol of hope for the future. Henry and Alice never had more children, but their household was often full of extended relatives and even orphans that Henry agreed to care for.

Everything seemed to be falling into place until 1861, when it all changed in the South. Major Holliday joined the Confederate army on October 31, 1861, serving under General P.G.T. Beauregard. In the major's absence, John Henry grew closer to his mother. Alice was determined that her son would be a Southern gentleman, and indeed it was a quality that stayed with him for the rest of his life. When she became sick, John Henry's feelings of protectiveness for his mother only increased.

General Beauregard

In the mid-19th century, tuberculosis was called consumption, a play on the fact that it seemed to eat away at the body until its victims literally drowned when their lungs could no longer function. It was not believed to be contagious, but rather hereditary, and the treatment prescribed to women was usually to stay home and perform their typical domestic duties, which essentially amounted to doing nothing different than perhaps eating a more bland diet. When the major returned to a war-torn Georgia after resigning his commission due to chronic diarrhea, Alice was weak and bedridden. He felt like he had no choice but to move his family as far from the war front as he could while still remaining in Georgia. Thus, in 1864, he moved them to Valdosta.

Once the Holliday family arrived in their new home, John Henry attended the Valdosta Institute for grammar school, receiving rigorous training in rhetoric and the classics from Samuel Varnedoe, a man credited with focusing more on achievement and nurturing of learning than disciplining with a switch. John Henry was a good student, well mannered, and popular with his classmates, and at home he was developing a close relationship with his older cousin, Mattie, whose family had come to Valdosta to join his own. His relationship with Mattie is just one of the great mysteries of his life. Some suggest that their relationship turned to romance, although there was never any confirmation of this. Either way, they did keep in contact throughout his life and he wrote to Mattie often. However, his world was turned upside down when his mother died from consumption on September 16, 1866.

John Henry was furious when 23 year-old neighbor Rachel Martin married his father three months later. To him, as well as to other members of the family, it was disrespectful to his mother's memory, and it was only made worse when Major Holliday moved his family from their farm to a house owned by his new in-laws. Others questioned the circumstances that would call for such a quick marriage. With a lawsuit filed against him by his former brother-in-law, who wanted his deceased sister's property back and questioned Henry's fidelity, Major Holliday's once close-knit family started to unravel.

Congressional candidate J.W. Clift visited the county courthouse to make a campaign speech on April 4, 1868. The courthouse happened to also be the headquarters for the Freedmen's Bureau, which was created in 1865 to assist former slaves with emergency food, shelter, medical care, and in some cases, family reunification. Major Holliday's appointment as an agent for the Freedmen's Bureau upset local citizens, as well as his son. When a small explosion went off during Clift's speech, John Henry was one of the young men suspected of involvement. Whether the young Holliday was actually involved is not known for sure, but it is known that Major Holliday's son was becoming angry and rebellious enough to do it.

John Henry Holliday, D.D.S.

Exactly why John Henry entered dental school is not clear, but chances are that he received some encouragement from his uncle, John Stiles Holliday, a respected physician who was living in Atlanta in 1869. Dr. Holliday was growing disillusioned with medicine and believed that dentistry was more respectable and, in many ways, more progressive. Dentists were already using anesthesia, while most doctors were still skeptical. Licensing standards for doctors were also loose, opening the door for scam artists selling questionable remedies. When Dr. Lucian Frink, a friend of Major Holliday's, agreed to be his preceptor, John Henry paid the $100 tuition and enrolled in Frink's alma mater, the Pennsylvania College of Dental Surgery.

Starting in October 1870, Holliday attended classes six days a week. The Valdosta Institute had prepared him well for the rigors of dental school. Chartered in 1856, the Pennsylvania College of Dental Surgery was one of the largest and most prestigious dental colleges in the world at the time, and in addition to attending lectures on topics such as chemistry, anatomy, and dental pathology, Holliday worked at the school's free clinic, which had developed an outstanding reputation for its dental care.

Holliday had never left Georgia before and, no doubt, Philadelphia was a new world for a young man who had been born and bred in the South. Holliday obviously went on to spend much of his life as a drinker and a gambler, and it would not be out of the realm of possibilities that he got his first exposure to these elements in Philadelphia. Still, Holliday was a good student. In March 1871, he returned to Valdosta to continue his training under Frink before going back to Philadelphia in September to complete his second year of studies. After writing his master's thesis, "Diseases of the Teeth," Holliday and 25 of his classmates attended graduation ceremonies and received their Doctor of Dental Surgery degrees.

It would be another five months before Holliday would receive his license to practice dentistry, because Georgia state law required that he be 21 years old and he was still only 20. In the meantime, he worked as an assistant to one of his classmates, A. Jameson Fuches, Jr., who opened a practice in St. Louis, Missouri.

The raucous river city offered Holliday more than professional experience. St. Louis was the home of a foster care runaway whose given name was Mary Katharine Harony. Born in Hungary, she had come to the U.S. and went by the name Kate Fisher, but in Western lore, she became best known by her nickname Big Nose Kate. Like many women of her time who had no family, she became a prostitute, and in 1872 she was living in a brothel and worked at a saloon not far from Dr. Fuches's office on Fourth Street.

Big Nose Kate (left) in 1865

Whether she started out as his girlfriend or he initially paid for her company, Kate and John Henry began their often-stormy relationship in St. Louis. Perhaps he was attracted to her courage, but her distrust of other people, especially of Wyatt Earp, would be a source of conflict in their relationship throughout much of Holliday's life. There is no evidence to support Kate's claim that they were married in Valdosta in 1876, but it is a fact that even though Holliday left St Louis without her in July 1872, it was far from the end of his time with Fisher.

Big Nose Kate, circa 1890

Holliday returned to Georgia just before his 21st birthday to claim the inheritance from his mother and then moved in with John Stiles Holliday in Atlanta, who by now had given up his medical practice for the grocery business. He renewed his friendship with his cousin, Robert, or Hub as he was known in the family, and the two handsome bachelors quickly established themselves in the Atlanta social scene. Hub would go on to become an esteemed dentist, graduating from the same school as John Henry, and he later helped found a dental college in Atlanta that was incorporated into Emory University in 1944.

John Stiles Holliday helped introduce his nephew to friends and associates in Atlanta with a party in the ballroom of his home and gave him a revolver just like the one he had given his three sons, an 1851 Colt revolver. The Holliday household in Atlanta also included Sophie Walton, the family's biracial servant. An expert card player who was adept with numbers, Sophie helped John Henry in his education as a gambler, providing information that would prove useful in the years that he would spend as a player and a dealer in the game of choice, faro. In the 19th century, Faro became one of the most popular gambling games in the U.S., especially in the West, where it was often called "Bucking the Tiger" because of the backs of early cards that featured a drawing of a Bengal Tiger.

Samuel Hape was also living with the Hollidays at that time. He had founded Atlanta Dental in 1868, and during the Civil War Hape was the only source of dental supplies for the Confederacy. He was acquainted with the dentist Arthur C. Ford and arranged for John Henry to have an interview with Dr. Ford. On July 26, 1872, Ford took out a notice in *The Atlanta Constitution* saying that Dr. John Holliday would be covering for him during his absence at a conference in August. Since Dr. Ford frequently had to travel, John Henry filled in for him on a regular basis.

Soon, John Henry became a landowner, assuming ownership of a building in Griffin that had belonged to his mother's family. When Hub had decided to quit dental school, thinking it was no longer necessary, John Henry talked him out of it and agreed to be Hub's preceptor at his alma mater. John Stiles promised financial assistance for the two young men to set up their practice together. Everything was aligning for John Henry Holliday to be a dentist and a respected member of Atlanta society.

Chapter 3: Wyatt Earp, Law Enforcer

Any thoughts Earp may have had about leading a stable, quite life in Missouri disappeared after the death of his wife and unborn child. Had he remained in Lamar, he would have needed to answer to lawsuits filed against him for misdeeds as town constable, including misusing funds. However, it did not take long for Earp to find more trouble as he headed back west. He was arrested in Van Buren, Arkansas in 1871 for stealing horses in Indian Territory but didn't stick around long enough for the trial, instead climbing out of the top of his jail cell and heading back to Illinois.

Finding himself on the run yet again, Earp traveled back west across the frontier, which by now was dotted with small cities and towns that had attracted the "Hell on Wheels" types. While all of the shady types posed problems for local law enforcement, Earp immersed himself in these cities, becoming notorious for being a regular patron of the saloons, gambling halls, and brothels that were in whatever town he had taken up temporary residence. That the young man would eventually become the West's most iconic figure would've made contemporaries of this time laugh, as they most often saw him in the company of prostitutes. At one point, he lived in a small, damp room on a floating brothel on the Illinois River, and it has even been suggested that Earp was a pimp, though whether or not this was true is not known for certain. Regardless, it is known that he was arrested several times for his involvement with prostitutes, and one working prostitute referred to herself as his wife for a period of time. Therefore, it should have surprised nobody when he eventually made his way to Kansas, where his brother, James, opened a brothel of his own.

James Earp

Earp had no trouble finding work in the raucous cattle town of Wichita during the summer. When cattle drivers came into town, the brothels of Wichita were busy, and Earp's skills as a bouncer came in handy when order needed to be restored. However, Earp found himself with little work to do in October 1874, so he accepted a job helping an off-duty Wichita policeman track down a wagon thief. After successfully locating the thieves and retrieving the stolen property, a positive article in the *Wichita Eagle* changed Earp's reputation. He was now publicly praised for a change, instead of being sued, chased, or otherwise vilified.

Buoyed by the positive press, Earp agreed to be a deputy marshal during summers in Wichita and later, in Dodge City. Unusually big for men of his era at 6 feet and 175 pounds, his physically intimidating methods were useful in dealing with the Texas cowboys who were in Dodge City to unwind. Though he would later become legendary for his deadly aim, Earp was proficient enough with his fists, and he learned on the job he did not need to fire a weapon to keep some type of order among the chaos. He was an efficient deputy and became a respected lawman in Kansas, often doing his work without even carrying a gun. In one of the times he did carry a gun, he inadvertently dropped it while leaning back in a chair, causing it to fire when it hit the ground and send a bullet through his coat. It may have been the first bullet to graze Earp's clothes, but it certainly wouldn't be the last.

Wyatt had rehabilitated his image and seemed to be finding a successful calling, but Marshal Earp was still courting controversy. During Wichita's election for city marshal on April 2, 1876, a former marshal accused Earp of using his office's powers to hire his brothers, a charge that led to Earp punching him out and publicly beating him. As a result, Wichita's lawman was arrested for disturbing the peace, bringing his stint as Marshal in Wichita to an abrupt end.

Chapter 4: Wyatt Earp and Doc Holliday Head West

Earp's Path to Tombstone

Wyatt's time in Wichita was over, but his career as a lawman certainly wasn't, and he didn't have to go far to find his next job. By 1876, Dodge City, Kansas had become a popular destination spot for cattle drives starting from as far south as Texas. It's known that Wyatt was appointed an assistant Marshal in Dodge City, but it's unclear how much time he spent there. It has been widely theorized that Earp even spent some time in the legendary frontier boomtown of Deadwood in the Black Hills of South Dakota, which is as popular as ever today thanks to the shooting of Wild Bill Hicock and a critically acclaimed HBO show about the town. It's also known that Wyatt spent some time in 1877 gambling down in Texas, and it was there that he met a man who would forever be associated with him, John Henry "Doc" Holliday.

Whatever the case, Earp made several famous acquaintances during his time in Dodge City, including with lawman Bat Masterson and prostitute Mattie Blaylock, who became his companion for several years. And on July 26, 1878, Earp was involved in his first famous shooting, which took place in the early morning after cowboy George Hoyt and a few other heavily intoxicated men shot their guns as they headed out of town on horseback. Earp, another policeman named James Masterson, and an untold number of citizens took aim at Hoyt and the others, and as the riders were crossing a bridge, Hoyt was shot in the arm, causing a wound that later developed into gangrene and killed him. Though it's not known who shot Hoyt, Wyatt was all too happy to take the credit, later claiming he fired the shot that hit him.

Mattie Blaylock

    By the time of the Hoyt shooting, Wyatt Earp was 30, and though he was still in good standing as an assistant marshal in Dodge City, he wanted something different for his life. He had witnessed the power of wealth each time cattle barons ended their cattle drives in Dodge City, and now he hoped to be able to trade in his badge for the opportunity to make some cash. Wyatt sensed the opportunity had come when his older brother Virgil contacted him about a silver strike in the rugged hills of southern Arizona Territory. Virgil Earp had been living in northern Arizona, serving in various law enforcement roles in the capital of Prescott, and when Virgil was appointed U.S. deputy marshal of Pima County in southern Arizona, he sent for his brothers, Wyatt and Morgan, to serve as special deputies to help him deal with the cowboys. With the lure of striking it rich in the silver mines, Wyatt Earp and Mattie Blaylock left Kansas in 1879 for the silver-mining boomtown of Tombstone, Arizona.

Virgil Earp

Doc Heads to Texas

Dr. Arthur Ford was not a well man. Like Holliday's mother, Dr. Ford was also suffering from consumption, and by New Year's Day 1873, Ford announced that he was going to Florida to recuperate. He turned his practice over to Dr. J. Cooper, not Holliday. Holliday had endured a difficult Christmas. His uncle (Mattie's father), Robert Holliday, died on Christmas Eve, and John Henry was with his family at the funeral. Weeks later, Francisco E'Dalgo, a Mexican orphan that lived with John Henry as a child, died from consumption. The next day, Holliday sold his half of the building he inherited from his mother in Griffin, pocketing $1,800. By the summer, he was in Dallas, Texas.

Why Holliday left Georgia for Dallas is another mystery and subject to much speculation. The most common theory is that he went west for his health. Bouts of coughing that got progressively worse into the winter of 1872 led to confirmation that Holliday, too, had consumption. There was no cure, nor was there really an effective treatment. Some said that Holliday was told to go west where the air is drier and, presumably, easier on his lungs. If there is a flaw to this theory, it is that Dallas can be quite humid and the weather is not that much different from Atlanta. If Holliday truly wanted to seek out dry air, he could have proceeded directly to the desert of the Southwest.

Another theory for his departure is that he was in love with his cousin, Mattie. It was not unheard of for first cousins to marry at the time, but Mattie was Catholic and her religion did not permit it. Certainly, they had a special relationship, but nobody would confirm that their relationship had ever turned to romance. Mattie burned some of the letters he wrote to her and another family member burned the rest of them years later. When he began to transform from Dr.

Holliday, the dentist, into Doc Holliday, the gunman, he still wrote to her even though by that time she was a nun.

A third theory, repeated by lawman turned journalist Bat Masterson, is that Holliday had committed murder and was forced to leave town. Few people deny that Holliday was involved in a shooting incident at swimming hole on the Withlacooche River near Valdosta. His uncle Tom McKey owned land near the river, and members of the family claimed a nearby swimming hole as their own. The African Americans who swam there had been advised to swim elsewhere. One day, a group of white men that included Holliday saw some young African Americans swimming there, despite previous warnings. Some say Holliday drew his Colt and shot over their heads, while others say he killed one, possibly three people. According to Masterson, Holliday said that his family advised him to go away for a while and helped him get to Dallas. Like other similar stories about Holliday, there is no documented evidence or record of the shooting, but that was not at all unusual for this period of history either. White violence against African Americans routinely occurred and went unreported, and it is also not unlikely that family members would sanitize the story, just as they might burn incriminating letters.

Whatever the cause, and perhaps it was a combination of all three theories, John Henry Holliday left his home state and headed west.

Bat Masterson

Dallas was not simply a random location to Holliday. He was acquainted with another dentist, Dr. John A. Seeger and became his partner in his practice in the summer of 1873. Seeger, a non-drinker, was probably pleased if Holliday's claim that he not only stopped drinking but also joined the local temperance society was true. Business was good for the young dentists, but once again, the partnership did not last long and ended the following March. Holliday's taste for whiskey and gambling had resurfaced, as did his illness. Indeed, the correlation between the desire for alcohol and the increasing coughing fits may have gone hand-in-hand.

Holliday was arrested in April 1874 for operating a keno game, but since he paid his property taxes on June 1, it appeared that he was still going to try and stay in Dallas. However, he left for Denison, an edgier, rougher town than Dallas, before the month was over, and it can be safely assumed that dentistry was taking a backseat to the allure of the gaming tables by now. Of course, Holliday may have been left with little choice; it is difficult to imagine that many people wanted a dentist with a persistent cough to treat them.

Regardless of how and why Holliday came to Denison, Holliday was starting to develop a reputation as a dangerous man, though the fact that so many of the stories about him are not supported by witnesses or documentation raises some questions. Certainly, it is not unusual if crimes in a more lawless time go unreported or if records were lost, but some historians have begun to question if Holliday spread the rumors about himself. The reasons may have simply been rooted in self-protection for a man, typically carrying a lot of cash, who often traveled alone through treacherous territory. Others believed that Holliday simply felt that he had little to lose because he knew he would not have a long life, even though he did look for treatment for his condition more than once.

Between 1875 and 1877, Holliday roamed across the West, and wherever he went, stories about shootings and other mayhem followed him. Known now as "Doc," but perhaps using the alias of Tom McKey, there were reports of him killing a solider in Jacksboro, Texas and cutting a man's face in Denver, Colorado. Some say he joined the goldrush in Deadwood, South Dakota, while still other reports placed him in Cheyenne, Wyoming before heading back to Texas. Wyatt Earp claims that Holliday was in Fort Griffin, Texas with Kate Fisher in 1877. Earp was there because he was on the trail of a band of outlaws known as The Trio. He never caught up with them – Bat Masterson eventually arrested them in Kansas in 1878 – but Earp did strike up a friendship with Holliday that became part of both men's legends.

Wyatt and Doc's Friendship

To a great extent, the lives of Doc Holliday and Wyatt Earp will forever be defined by a 30-second gun battle in Tombstone, Arizona, which Earp would spend his final years trying to forget. Holliday was there, too, even though Earp told him he didn't need to be. In fact, no stories about Earp in Tombstone are complete without Holliday. However, Holliday has come to be viewed by many as Earp's sidekick, which is not accurate. Masterson wrote of Holliday in "Human Life" magazine in 1907, "His whole heart and soul were wrapped up in Wyatt Earp..."[1] Holliday was a good friend to Earp and raised to be loyal to his friends, but he was nobody's sidekick.

They met in a saloon in Fort Griffin, but their friendship took hold in Dodge City, Kansas. Upon leaving Texas, Holliday wrote to Mattie in 1878 that he had "enjoyed as much of this as [I] could stand."[2] Earp, as tall as Holliday but much more physically intimidating, aspired to make some cash more than he aspired to be a lawman. Still, he was respected as deputy marshal of Dodge City, which needed a man like Earp to help keep order when the Texas cowboys were in town to blow off steam.

By 1876, Dodge City, Kansas had become a popular destination spot for cattle drives starting from as far south as Texas, and though it's known that Wyatt was appointed an assistant Marshal in Dodge City, but it's unclear how much time he spent there. It has been widely theorized that Earp even spent some time in the legendary frontier boomtown of Deadwood in the Black Hills of South Dakota, which is as popular as ever today thanks to the shooting of Wild Bill Hicock and a critically acclaimed HBO show about the town. It's also known that Wyatt spent some time in 1877 gambling down in Texas, which is where he first met Holliday.

Masterson was the sheriff when Holliday arrived and claimed to tolerate Holliday and his stories more out of respect for Earp than for any good feelings about Doc. Masterson thought that Holliday was dangerous and perhaps a little crazy. When Masterson became a writer, he wrote about Holliday, "He was selfish and had a perverse nature – traits not calculated to make a man popular in the early days of the frontier."[3]

Clearly, Holliday's reputation had preceded him before he arrived in Dodge City, and according to Earp, Holliday's departure from Fort Griffin was hastened by an incident at a poker game involving a man named Ed Bailey. Holliday reportedly advised Bailey to stop playing with the pile of discarded cards, called deadwood, and focus more on the game, which was a way of politely asking him to stop cheating. When Bailey continued to cheat, Holliday whipped out a knife that he always carried and stabbed the man. When Holliday took off to his room, Kate deliberately set a shed on fire to create a diversion and the two escaped to Kansas. Whether the incident really happened the way Earp, who was not a witness, told it or whether it even happened in Texas, nobody knows, but it did contribute to Holliday's reputation as a man who would kill you before he backed down.

---

[1] "Bat Masterson Not Impressed by Doc Holliday." *Territorial News.* December 15, 2010.
[2] Gary L. Roberts. *Doc Holliday: The Life and Legend.* Page 89.
[3] *Territorial News*

Earp also claimed that it was this streak in Holliday that saved Earp's life in 1878 and cemented their friendship. Earp said that he found himself surrounded by outlaws somewhere near the Long Branch Saloon on Dodge City's famous Front Street. Holliday was nearby at a gaming table and saw the men closing in on Earp. After asking the card dealer if he could borrow his six-shooter, Holliday bolted for the door, drew both his own gun and the borrowed gun, and ordered the outlaws to put up their hands. Earp said this gave him time to draw his own gun and place the men under arrest.

Doc Heads to Las Vegas, New Mexico

Initially, at least, Holliday felt a sense of acceptance in Dodge City that eluded him in Texas. Certainly the environment in the dusty cowtown suited him, with enough saloons and faro tables to keep him entertained. The very existence of Dodge City, located in western Kansas, was tied to the state Holliday had left behind. Wealthy cattle barons from Texas passed through and, in many cases, left both their cattle and their cash in Dodge City. The more saloons, brothels, and gaming tables there were, the more opportunity there was for the businessmen of Dodge City to make a profit.

One thing that Dodge City did not have when Holliday arrived was a dentist, prompting him to take out an advertisement in *The Dodge City Times* on June 8, 1878. He offered his dentistry services to the community, with a money-back guarantee. His office was located in Room 24 at the Dodge House Hotel, adjacent to a billiards hall. Holliday even had a pocket dental kit, complete with the basic dental tools of the day, and an inscription with his name and the address of his office. All of this suggests that Holliday might have considered settling down in Kansas.

As it turned out, Holliday did not settle down. He was more successful as a gambler than a dentist, and the dust of Dodge City did little to help his health. His cough was deep and persistent, while his voice had become hoarse due to ulcers in his throat, which often made it hard for him to speak above a whisper. He lost more weight and his color alternated between red and pale. The humidity of Kansas was also no help, but there was word that the Montezuma Hot Springs in Gallinas Canyon in New Mexico had helped others suffering from consumption.

The timing was right to move on if Holliday desired to do so. Dodge City's prime cattle running season was coming to an end with winter just around the corner. The town was also trying to get a handle on prostitution and gambling, and on August 6, 1878 it passed ordinances outlawing both. They were not truly outlawed as the town wanted to regulate the big moneymakers, not eliminate them, but the result was making it more expensive and difficult for a man like Holliday to gamble. Holliday also claimed to be falsely implicated in a robbery at a local store, so with these factors in mind, he and Kate moved on to Las Vegas, New Mexico in the winter of 1878.

They made it as far as Trinidad, Colorado when the snow began to fall. With Doc's health failing, the faced a difficult decision. They either stayed in brutally cold Trinidad or risked Holliday deteriorating even more on the road. Ultimately, they hired a teamster who was on his way to Santa Fe to transport Kate and a very ill Doc to Las Vegas by rail. Doc and Kate arrived in Las Vegas just before Christmas 1878, referring to themselves as Dr. and Mrs. J.H. Holliday. It may have been simply easier to explain their relationship this way even if Kate was just his common-law wife. Northwest of the town plaza was the mecca for consumption patients, 22 springs at the base of the mountains that produced water ranging in temperatures from 110 degrees up to 140 degrees. Las Vegas was full of people, most young and mostly wealthy, who had come to these springs, hoping for a cure for their consumption. They called themselves the Lungers Club.

After settling in, Holliday opened a dental practice in an office not far from the town plaza. He shared space with jeweler and watchmaker, William Leonard, another young man afflicted with consumption. Holliday, already well-acquainted with men with questionable pasts, was not put off by the story that Leonard shot Jose Mares the previous fall in front of a local store and then took a beating from Mares' friends. They developed a friendship that lasted until Leonard was indicted on charges and left town.

Holliday began to recover his strength in Las Vegas and soon felt well enough to open a saloon. However, neither the record-breaking frigid temperatures nor the new law that would prohibit gambling within New Mexico Territory would help Holliday's income as dentist or a saloonkeeper/gambler. He was fined $25 for running a monte table in March 1879, prompting him to head back to Dodge City, this time without Kate. Holliday made a little money there helping Masterson organize a group of fighters for the Atchison, Topeka, & Santa Fe Railroad. The railroad had asked Sheriff Masterson to help fight off attacks on workers in a contested pass at Canon City, Colorado. Holliday did a bit more work for the railroad before he went back to Las Vegas.

By this time, Las Vegas was preparing for the arrival of the railroad, which ultimately bypassed the town by about a mile. Still, businesses were being built, plans were being made and many of the gamblers that Holliday knew from Dodge City followed the line into town. Trouble followed him, too. He was accused of shooting a man named Mike Gordon, who opened gunfire when one of the saloon girls turned down his advances. There were reports of other trouble, too, but like many of the tales about Holliday, it is not known if they ever occurred.

Holliday may have wanted to stay in Las Vegas, but he was soon on the road again. Wyatt Earp and his common-law wife, Mattie, had come to town, talking about a silver strike in Arizona. With the lure of striking it rich in the silver mines, Wyatt Earp and Mattie Blaylock left Kansas in 1879 for the silver-mining boomtown of Tombstone, Arizona. After a stop in Albuquerque, Holliday headed west again, this time for Arizona.

Chapter 5: Becoming Legends in Arizona

Wyatt Strikes Out

Tombstone in 1881

While Wyatt Earp was deputy marshal of Dodge City in 1877, Ed Schieffelin was working for the U.S. government as an Indian scout in Arizona. After leaving the Grand Canyon area, Schieffelin moved south and was stationed at Fort Huachuca, not far from the Mexican border. As he was known to do, Schieffelin went out on his own to search for "rocks." Other soldiers in the camp told him that the only stone he would find out in the rugged hills was his tombstone. When he found silver, the soon-to-be millionaire named his first mine "The Tombstone."

Schieffelin

As word of Schieffelin's discovery spread, prospectors streamed into the camp near where he had staked his claim. The tents soon gave way to buildings, and when the national census was taken in 1880, Tombstone had 2,100 residents. By the time a special census was taken in Arizona in 1882 to accounting for the new counties that had sprung up in the past two years, Tombstone reported 5,300 residents, second only to Tucson. At its peak, as many as 15,000 people crowded Tombstone's dusty streets.

Few, if any, people paid attention to the wagon that carried Earp and Mattie into town in December 1879. Only a few hundred people lived there at the time the Earp family arrived to join Virgil, but the signs of growing wealth were there. Soon there would be churches, restaurants, and shops, some of which were even indicative of the sophistication of the Victorian Era. These symbols of the times often stood in stark contrast to the dusty mines nearby. The Earps had come to Tombstone to cash in like everybody else, but even at this time, Tombstone was quickly becoming the domain of more sophisticated mining companies from cities such as New York, San Francisco, or London. Little was left to small, individual prospectors, even as the town's population exploded over the next several years, and any hopes of getting rich off of the silver mines were short-lived.

Wyatt Earp's rather short retirement from law enforcement ended when he accepted a job as shotgun rider for Wells Fargo. His job was to protect the content of the strongbox under the driver's seat. Weighing up to 150 pounds and made of oak, pine, and iron, the strongboxes containing gold, cash, and other valuables were natural targets for thieves. Earp was glad to leave the job in the summer of 1880, and with his other business ventures having already failed so quickly, he became a deputy sheriff of Tombstone. As was the case in Kansas, Earp was good at his work, a fact that was appreciated by the people of Tombstone. Being in law enforcement in Tombstone was made more challenging, though, by the fact that the authorities in Arizona paid little attention to what the local cowboys did in Mexico.

Doc Heads to Tombstone

Prescott, Arizona bore little resemblance to Tombstone. The northern Arizona town was the capital, lost the title to Tucson in 1867, then got it back again in 1877 before losing it for good to Phoenix in 1889. As the capital city, it was busy and had its share of gambling halls and saloons along famed Whiskey Row. However, it was not a boomtown and lacked the edginess of Tombstone.

Earp had invited Holliday to join him in Tombstone, which stayed in Holliday's mind as he gambled and walked the streets of Prescott. They had arrived in Prescott together in November 1879 and immediately went to see Virgil and Allie Earp, who had been Prescott residents for two years when they told Wyatt about the silver strike. When Jim, Virgil, and Wyatt Earp and their families were ready to go to Tombstone about a week later, where they planned to meet their brother, Morgan, Holliday had already found the gambling scene in Prescott to his liking. He was on a hot streak, so he and Kate opted to stay. This suited Kate just fine as she never really liked Wyatt and did not want Doc to be around him, either.

Kate and Doc's relationship was littered with turbulent periods resulting in frequent separations. One of those periods appears to have come at some point in their stay in Prescott because the 1880 census listed Holliday as a single man. One of his roommates at the boarding house where he lived was John J. Gosper, who happened to be the acting governor of Arizona in General John C. Fremont's absence. No doubt Holliday and Gosper had interesting discussions on the point of alcohol, considering that Gosper was an active member of the temperance society and Holliday was an active indulger of whiskey. Soon, though, Holliday would be on the move again.

Whether it was due to the end of his hot streak at the tables or due to strong recruitment effort by Wyatt, it was September 1880 when Holliday finally arrived in Tombstone, according to voter registration records. Kate, irritated at Doc for reuniting with the Earps, went to Globe, Arizona instead.

When Holliday arrived, Tombstone was still rough around the edges, but it was still also quite a bit different than the town that the Earps rolled into the previous December. Prospector tents from miners looking for the motherlode had given way to permanent buildings and the census shot up from a few hundred when the Earps arrived to 2,100 in 1880. A special census in Arizona in 1882, made necessary by the new counties that were created over the previous two years, indicated that Tombstone's population had grown to 5,300. At one point, it would swell to 15,000 people.

It did not take long for the town to be invaded by wealthy businessmen and entrepreneurs. Their wives could be seen dressed in their finest Victorian dresses, walking along the dusty sidewalks or playing lawn tennis at posh hotels that butted up against the town's dirty mines. Any hopes of individual prospectors, such as the Earps, cashing in were quickly dashed when larger, better financed mining companies from the likes of New York and San Francisco moved into town to strip the mountains of their silver.

Businessmen weren't the only ones making their way to Tombstone. Though cowboys have been historically associated with courage and heroism, to call someone a cowboy at this time was an insult. Ranching and herding were legitimate professions, but a cowboy was a thief. Given its proximity to the border, Tombstone attracted its share of cowboys, who went into Mexico to steal cattle (often murdering innocent Mexicans in the process) and then brought the cattle to Tombstone to sell them to legitimate ranchers. This did not sit well with the businesses that owned the mines. The corporate - and largely Republican - establishment that had come to Tombstone to make money wanted the Earps to keep order. Arizona was still a territory and could not expect to achieve statehood, nor could the corporations expect to attract investors, if chaos and lawlessness reigned. Thus, despite hoping to leave law enforcement behind, Wyatt soon found himself needing work, and by the summer of 1880, he was deputy sheriff in Tombstone.

The Oriental Saloon

The Oriental Saloon was not only the most luxurious saloon and gambling hall in Tombstone, it was one of the finest in the entire West, making it a natural place for Holliday to frequent. On July 22, 1880, The Tombstone Daily Epitaph reported about the Saloon:

> "Last evening the portals were thrown open and the public permitted to gaze upon the most elegantly furnished saloon this side of the Golden Gate. Twenty-eight burners suspended in neat chandeliers afforded an illumination of ample brilliancy and the bright rays reflected from the many colored crystals in the bar sparkled like a December icing in the sunshine. The saloon comprises two apartments. To the right of the main entrance is the bar, beautifully carved, finished in white and gilt and capped with a handsomely polished top. In the rear of this stand a brace of sideboards....They were made for the Baldwin Hotel, of San Francisco....The back apartment is covered with a brilliant body brussels [sic] carpet and suitably furnished after the style of a grand club room, with conveniences for the wily dealers in polished ivory....Tombstone has taken the lead and [to] Messrs. Joyce and Co. our congratulations."

When Holliday arrived, the town was experiencing a gambling war between the so-called Easterners, gamblers who came from east of the Pacific Coast, and the Slopers, mostly from California. Wyatt had recently been given an interest in the Oriental's gambling hall, providing him with a cut of the concessions in exchange for helping keep order among the gamblers who hoped to disrupt the town's gambling arrangements.

One of the men doing the disrupting was John E. Tyler from Jackson County, Missouri. Tyler got into trouble in Tombstone on September 23, 1880 when he got into an argument with a gambler associated with the Easterners, but others jumped in and defused the situation before it got out of hand. On October 10, it was Holliday's turn to tussle with Tyler. The two men, unarmed due to the city ordinance against carrying a concealed weapon, got into an argument. Milton Joyce, who leased the bar and was the saloonkeeper that night, helped separate the two men and ordered them to leave. Tyler left, but Holliday began to argue with Joyce. With little effort, Joyce, a much larger man than Holliday, physically removed him from the bar and deposited him into the street.

Joyce

Holliday's pistol had been checked behind the bar and when he walked back into the Oriental to ask for it, Joyce refused. Undeterred, Holliday went to his room at Fly's boardinghouse, got another pistol and went back to the Oriental with his gun drawn. Joyce came out from behind the bar with a gun and may have shot it once, but definitely used it to give Holliday a beating, prompting many to think that Holliday was surely going to die. Shots were fired from all corners by this point and one hit Joyce in the hand. When it was obvious Doc's wounds were not critical, Holliday was arrested and paid a $30 fine. The incident was not over, though, and neither was the feud. The following May, he was indicted by the Grand Jury and after a continuance, a trial was scheduled for October 6, 1881. Holliday would never appear for the trial.

For a time after that, Holliday managed to stay out of legal trouble, focusing his interests on mining properties, acquiring water rights, and, of course, gambling. Kate visited him more than once to try to persuade him to return to Globe with her, where she had opened a hotel. Still harboring bad feelings for the Earps, she no doubt made her feelings known because on at least one occasion, their argument resulted in Doc getting arrested. Her attempts to separate Doc from the Earps only served to drive a wedge in her own relationship with him.

Wyatt's Early Law Enforcement Career in Tombstone

The Earps, by virtue of their role as enforcers for the Republican establishment, were never truly accepted by the community of Democratic ranchers. They were respected for their role, but they were still widely viewed as outsiders. Wyatt's tendency to frequent saloons and gambling halls also raised some eyebrows, as did his friendship with Holliday.

Perhaps not surprisingly, Wyatt quickly found himself caught up in adventure, and controversy, on the job. On October 28, 1880, Tombstone marshal Fred White headed to Allen Street to break up a group of intoxicated men shooting their guns into the air, apparently at the Moon. As White grabbed the pistol of an outlaw cowboy named Curly Bill Brocius, it went off, hitting White in the groin. Wyatt, seeing the start of the confrontation, commandeered someone's pistol and pistol-whipped Curly Bill, all while Curly Bill's friends started shooting at him. White died days later, and even though the Earps likely saved Curly Bill's life by taking him into custody before the mob got hold of him, he remained permanently bitter about being pistol-whipped, and he was implicated by at least one person in the murder of Morgan Earp in March 1882. Curly Bill had become Arizona's most famous outlaw after the shooting of White, but his reign would be short. Less than two years later, Curly Bill would die in a shootout at the hands of none other than Wyatt Earp.

Curly Bill

When the news came from Prescott in Spring 1881 that Tombstone was going to be the seat of Cochise County, Wyatt liked his chances at being named sheriff, which was also a profitable position because the sheriff collected the taxes (and Wyatt already had a history of "misusing" funds and having others go missing). He assumed that being from the North would carry some weight with the Republican governor, John C. Fremont, as would the fact that he was more aligned with the town's business interests, but when it became obvious to Earp that Fremont planned to appoint Democrat Johnny Behan, he withdrew from consideration. Earp also claimed that Behan promised to make him the undersheriff, but this never happened.

Behan

The rivalry for sheriff was not the only thing that Earp and Behan shared. Both men were interested in the affections of 18 year old Josephine "Sadie" Marcus, even though Earp was still involved with Mattie Blaylock. It seems as though Earp was on his way to losing this battle too, at least until Josephine caught Behan in bed with another woman in 1881. Eventually, Earp and Josephine developed their own romance, as Mattie Blaylock descended into drug addiction.

Sadie

The Origins of the Feud with the Clantons and McLaurys

The situation between Earp and Behan did not improve when a Wells Fargo stagecoach on its way to Tombstone from Benson, Arizona was robbed on March 15, 1881. The robbers got away with $26,000, and the driver and a passenger were murdered. Holliday's troubles with Milt Joyce, as well as his trouble with Kate, resurfaced when Kate went back to Tombstone in July. Once again, Kate and Doc argued and Kate turned to alcohol to console herself. Behan and Joyce came across Kate in her drunken condition and suggested a way for her to get back at it Holliday. She swore an affidavit saying that Doc had committed the robbery in Benson. She later said, "I became desperate and in a vain hope of breaking up their [the Earps] association with Doc, whom I loved...I had known I was taking a desperate chance, and I was not astonished when I lost out."[4]

Behan arrested Holliday on July 5, but the case was dropped on July 9. Not a shred of evidence existed to implicate Holliday, but the incident stayed in the minds of many. As for Kate, Doc sent her on her way back to Globe. Meanwhile, the actual killers had yet to be caught and Wells Fargo was unhappy. The company personally insured all cargo and needed to regain the trust of its customers. They wanted the bandits, dead or alive, and they wanted an example made of them. Sheriff Behan organized one posse and Virgil organized another, which included Holliday, Wyatt, and Masterson. Virgil Earp's posse tracked down a man who admitted to holding horses while the robbery occurred and they turned the man over to Behan. The man later escaped from jail, but the Earps claimed that Behan let him go.

---

[4] Reynolds, 155.

Wyatt Earp still had his mind set on getting the sheriff's office and thought that the stagecoach robbery could help, albeit indirectly. He worked out a deal with Ike Clanton, who was well acquainted with the cowboys that made their way in and out of Tombstone. Earp was confident that the cowboys knew who pulled off the robbery and if he could get enough information and solve the case, it seemed like he could score enough political points to become sheriff. Earp offered Clanton $6,000 for his help, which Clanton could not turn down. However, his only condition was that Earp keep the deal a secret. He knew if the cowboys found out about his betrayal, they would kill him. Wyatt later testified that he had also offered a reward to Frank McLaury for information about the identities of the cowboys, and Ike Clanton would later testify that Wyatt had admitted the Earps and Holliday were involved in the robbery themselves.

Clanton never got the chance to collect because the three cowboys that were responsible for the robbery and murder were killed in New Mexico after getting mixed up in a barroom brawl, but the secret between Earp and Clanton remained.

Ike Clanton

Harboring this secret did not ease Clanton's mind. He was convinced that Earp told Holliday about the arrangement, but Earp denied it. Clanton tried to goad Earp into admitting that he told Holliday by saying that Doc himself said he knew about the deal. Holliday was in Tucson when, on October 21, Wyatt sent Morgan to get him and ask him to return to Tombstone. Wyatt wanted to ask Holliday himself what, if anything, he knew. When Holliday arrived, he assured Wyatt he knew nothing about a deal between him and Ike Clanton, who had briefly left town to tend to other business.

Throughout the middle months of 1881, the resentment between the Earps and McLaurys also began to mount. When another stagecoach was robbed near Tombstone on September 8, it was determined that the robbers were Pete Spence and Frank Stilwell, both friends of the McLaury brothers. After they were arrested and released on bail, Virgil Earp arrested the pair again on October 13, either for a different charge or for a different robbery, but the McLaurys believed that Earp was harassing the two and arresting them for the same charge as before. Frank McLaury warned Morgan Earp that if the Earps arrested the McLaurys or their friends again, they were dead men.

Frank McLaury

On October 25, 1881, Clanton returned to Tombstone with Tom McLaury. The more he drank, the more his paranoia got the best of him. The more paranoid he got, the more he talked, and several people said they heard him make threats about killing Wyatt. When Holliday saw Clanton at the Alhambra Saloon, he directly confronted him and suggested that he stop saying that Earp had betrayed him. By now, Clanton was extremely drunk and continued his threats. Holliday responded by calling Clanton a liar. The incident was on the verge of escalating into a gunfight when Virgil intervened and threatened to arrest them both.

When Clanton saw Wyatt later in the evening, he told him he would get him in the morning. Wyatt ignored Clanton and went home to bed. Clanton, however, did not go to bed. He made his way to the Oriental for more drinking and a poker game with Behan, and, of all people, Virgil, who played cards that night with a pistol lying across his lap.

The Gunfight at the O.K. Corral

The O.K. Corral in 1882

When the Earps and Holliday woke up the next morning, October 26, 1882, they were told that Ike Clanton was walking the streets of Tombstone, going from saloon to saloon to announce his intentions to kill them. Some said Clanton went into the telegraph office to wire for help, and the town began to buzz with concern that a gang of angry cowboys was about to descend on Tombstone. Holliday could not help but hear the rumors and went to help. Earp told him, "This is none of your affair," to which Holliday said, "That is a hell of thing to say to me."[5] After the events that followed, many questioned why Holliday, known to have a quick temper, would be asked to help disarm the Clantons and the McLaurys, if that was Virgil Earp's intention.

In addition to Clanton's threats, Wyatt got into a physical confrontation with Tom McLaury, pistol-whipping him outside the courthouse after Tom had told him he was unarmed despite plainly and visibly carrying a revolver tucked near his right hip. It was for this reason that the Earps may have assumed Tom was armed when the gunfight started hours later.

No mob of angry cowboys ever appeared, but by the early afternoon, Ike Clanton had been joined by his brother Billy, cowboy Billy Claiborne, and Frank and Tom McLaury. The group of five were standing in a vacant lot on Fremont Street near the rear of the O.K. Corrall, in close proximity to where Holliday was renting a room and on the route to the homes of the Earps, possibly intending to serve a threatening warning to them. Around 2:30 p.m., Sheriff Behan attempted to persuade the cowboys to disarm themselves, but his request was quickly rejected.

---

[5] Roberts, 194.

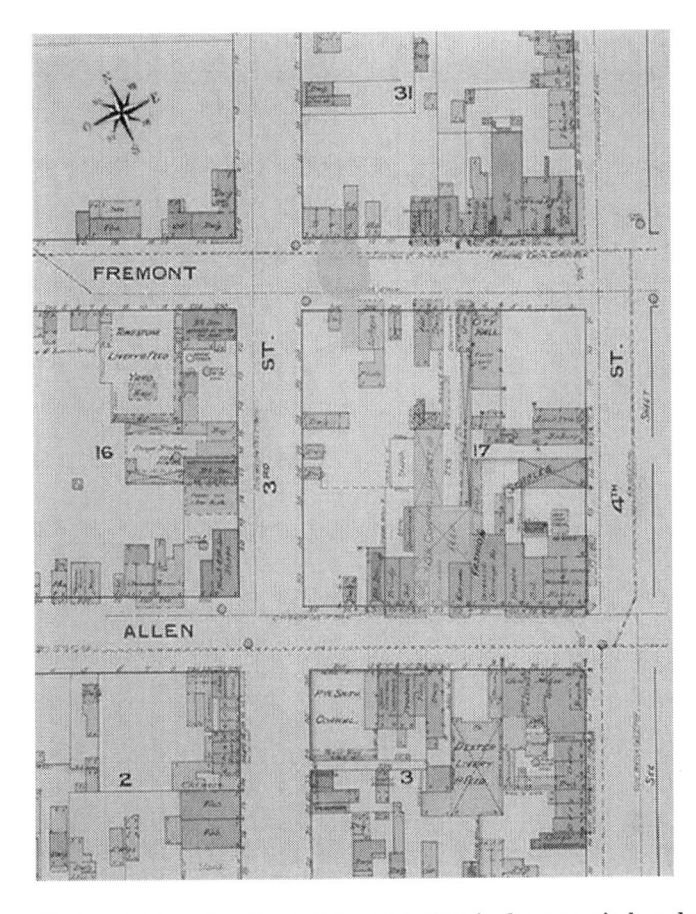

The O.K. Corral is in yellow. The fighting took place in the green circle and alley

At about 3:00 p.m., Wyatt, Morgan, and Virgil Earp, along with Holliday, headed to the lot to confront the cowboys. The Earps were carrying revolvers, while Holliday had a pistol and a shotgun given to him by Virgil, which he had concealed under his long coat to avoid alarming the citizens of Tombstone.

Despite the fact that the most famous gunfight in American history took place moments later, exactly how it all went down remains heavily disputed and not completely clear. The Earps claimed that Virgil approached the Clantons and the McLaurys, stopping within a few feet of them to inform them that they were under arrest. Some say that Billy Clanton and Frank

McLaury were about to surrender, while the Earps claimed that the two went for their guns. One resident, Martha J. King, claimed the Earps told Holliday to "let them have it" and initiated the gunfight.

Who started the shooting was disputed, but everyone agreed that two shots were fired almost simultaneously, touching off the firing. However it started, the gunfight lasted, by all accounts, about 30 seconds. When it was over, an unarmed Ike Clanton and Billy Claiborne had run away, but the McLaury brothers, including an unarmed Tom, were dead in the street. Billy Clanton had suffered a painful and fatal gunshot wound to the chest, still slumping near the corner of the Macdonald house, where he had been leaning when the shooting started. Virgil and Morgan Earp were wounded, as was Holliday. It is believed that Billy Clanton and Frank McLaury, even after being wounded, continued shooting, and one of them hit Morgan Earp across the back. Virgil thought Billy Clanton hit him in the calf and began firing at him after being injured. Frank McLaury hit Holliday in a pocket and grazed him, incensing him and leading him to chase after Frank shouting, "That son of a bitch has shot me, and I am going to kill him." Wyatt managed to walk away without so much as a scratch. According to Big Nose Kate, when Holliday came back to his room he openly wept, stating, "That was awful—awful."

Tom McLaury

In Tombstone, the initial reaction after the gunfight was that the Earps and Holliday were heroes. *The Tombstone Epitaph*'s described the shootout, "Wyatt Earp stood up and fired in rapid succession, as cool as a cucumber, and was not hit." The *San Francisco Examiner* suggested that Tombstone's residents be grateful to have the Earps on their side of the law.

However, that sentiment did not last long. Plenty of people in Tombstone believed that the three dead men were murdered in cold blood, and they wondered why the Earps would ever ask a hothead like Doc Holliday to help them disarm the McLaurys and the Clantons. The local undertaker displayed the three corpses in their coffins in his window with a sign that read, "Murdered in the Streets of Tombstone."

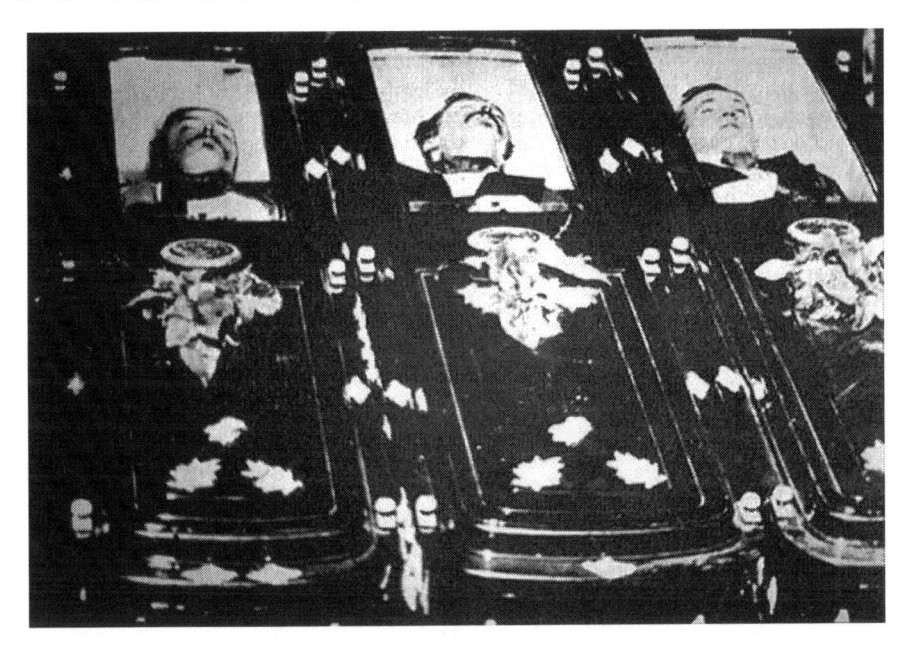

The corpses of Tom McLaury, Frank McLaury, and Billy Clanton were publicly displayed in the undertaker's window.

Ike Clanton filed murder charges against Holliday and the Earps. Wyatt and Doc spent 16 days in jail, while Virgil Earp was temporarily suspended as town marshal. Just over a month after the shootout, the case was brought before Justice Wells Spicer. Ultimately, he found in favor of the defendants, determining that there was too little evidence to indict the defendants and that the evidence that did exist suggested they had acted within the law. Still, the ruling further incensed many people in Tombstone and left Ike Clanton still wanting revenge. The tension and assassination threats directed at the Earps were enough to lead the federal government to take notice, particularly because the cowboys continued to run amok unchecked in Mexico and the government wanted to avoid an international incident.

The Earps Become Targets

It took little time for Clanton to get his revenge. On December 28, 1881, Virgil was ambushed in the street and shot in the arm by a shotgun blast as he left the Oriental Hotel. The shooter had hidden in drugstore that was under construction across the street. The force of the shot spun Virgil around and blew his arm into two, but he did not leave his feet until collapsing into Wyatt's arms back across the street. He would have no use of the arm for the rest of his life.

The shooter was never identified, but Ike Clanton's hat was found near where the shots had been fired. Clanton was later acquitted after several eyewitnesses testified he was not in Tombstone at the time of the shooting. In response to the attack on Virgil, Wyatt requested from the U.S. Marshal Crawley Dake that he be appointed a deputy U.S. marshal and given the ability to choose his own deputies, a request that was granted. The Earps racked up such expenses while bolstering their protection and swelling their ranks that Wyatt later had to mortgage his own house, and it was foreclosed on after he failed to repay the debt.

A few months after the attempt on Virgil's life, the Earp brothers' luck ran out. A few months later, in March 1882, Morgan Earp was playing pool in a billiards hall after attending a theater show. As he was playing, gunmen entered an alley outside the building and fired into the room, hitting Morgan in the spine. Wyatt was nearly hit by one of the bullets himself, which went straight over his head. As the gunmen escaped into the night, Morgan died within the hour.

Morgan Earp

The Earp Vendetta Ride

Now it was the Earps and Holliday's turn to seek revenge. Two days after Morgan's death, which happened to be Wyatt's 34th birthday, the grieving Wyatt made arrangements for Morgan's body to be sent to their father's home in Colma, California. Morgan was reportedly buried in a suit that belonged to Holliday. Virgil and his wife, Allie, left for San Francisco under the watchful eye of armed guards, and Holliday joined Wyatt when it was time for Virgil and Allie to board the train from Tucson to San Francisco.

As the train left the station in Tucson, Wyatt claimed to have seen Ike Clanton and Frank Stilwell lying in wait for Virgil. After a brief chase, Clanton got away, but Wyatt shot and killed Stilwell, leaving his body riddled with bullets by the railroad tracks. Though it was just days after the attack on Morgan, Wyatt may already have believed that Stilwell was one of the men who shot at Morgan. Pete Spence's wife later claimed that Spence and Stilwell were among a group of men who had returned home shortly after Morgan had been shot, and that Spence had threatened to harm her if she told authorities anything.

Stilwell

While Wyatt and his posse, which included Holliday and his brother Warren, continued its search for Morgan's killers, Sheriff Behan put together his own posse to search for Earp, now wanted for Stilwell's murder. Just before conducting his infamous month long "vendetta ride", Wyatt had a famous confrontation with Behan, who sought to meet with him, warning the sheriff, "Johnny, if you're not careful you'll see me once too often."

Warren Earp

Before Behan could find him, the vendetta posse killed a cowboy named Florentino Cruz, also known as Indian Charlie, based on a rumor that he was involved in killing Morgan. Soon thereafter, the posse killed Curley Bill Brocius, Wyatt's nemesis from a few years earlier, though there was no evidence that Bronchus was involved with Morgan's death. The lawless vendetta to avenge the killing of Morgan quickly erased any support he may have had from the residents or businesses of Tombstone.

By the time the Earp Vendetta Ride was over, the posse had killed four outlaws. On April 13, 1882, Earp and Sadie Marcus left Arizona and went to Gunnison, Colorado to weather the storm. Mattie had already left for California and was with Virgil and his family. Wyatt expected the same businessmen who had financed him on his "Vendetta Ride" to come through and work out a pardon for the crimes he had committed so he could return to Tombstone and run for sheriff. But by this time many in Tombstone were glad to have him gone, and after six months of waiting it was apparent that a pardon would never come. Earp and his new common-law wife, who would remain with him for the rest of his life, went west again and headed to San Francisco.

Wanted for murder and with little, if any, support from the town, it was time for Earp and Holliday to leave Arizona in Spring 1882. It was also time for the friends to part ways. Mattie Earp was already in California with Virgil, where she would wait in vain for Wyatt to return. He may not have become sheriff, but he did get Behan's woman, and Sadie Marcus would remain with Wyatt for the rest of his life. Earp and his new common-law wife headed to San Francisco, while Doc Holliday stayed in Colorado.

Chapter 6: Doc Holliday's Final Years

Holliday could not have returned to Arizona if he wanted to, at least not without facing a possible death sentence, but when he arrived in Denver in May 1882, he was arrested for Stilwell's murder. Behan made it clear that if Holliday appeared back in Tombstone, he would see to it that Holliday hanged and called for his extradition back to Arizona. With some intervention from Wyatt, who called on his old friend and the sheriff of Trinidad, Colorado, Bat Masterson, the extradition was blocked. Masterson had pulled some political strings, which evidently went as high as the governor's office.

The seminal moments associated with Holliday were now behind him, but Holliday's final years were marked by much of the same events as the prior 15 years of his life. He followed the gambling circuit around Colorado as his health permitted, never quite able to escape his reputation or bloodshed. Holliday and Wyatt were falsely accused of killing the cowboy Johnny Ringo, a friend of Ike Clanton's and Frank Stilwell's, in Arizona, though neither men were anywhere near the state at the time. It's possible that Doc was implicated simply because of the bad blood that previously existed between him and Ringo. In Tombstone in January 1882, only 3 months after the Shootout at the O.K. Corral, Holliday got into a heated argument with Ringo and allegedly said, "All I want of you is ten paces out in the street." A duel was stopped only by Tombstone's police, who arrested both of them.

Ringo

Though Doc almost certainly had nothing to do with Ringo's murder, Doc did indeed shoot Billy Allen in the arm over a $5 debt in 1884. This case actually went to trial, but on March 28, 1885, the jury believed that Doc had acted in self-defense, even if there was little evidence to support this.

The altitude of Colorado was not good for a man with consumption, and any gains he made in his battle against the disease in New Mexico and Arizona were soon wiped away in the Rocky Mountains. With his hair now gray, his body wasting away, and a growing dependence on alcohol to ease his misery, Holliday had a reunion with Earp in a hotel lobby in Denver in May 1885. Sadie watched the meeting from across the room, and both she and Wyatt were shocked at Holliday's appearance. When they parted, there were tears in Wyatt's eyes. Later in Denver, Holliday also ran into his old nemesis, Milt Joyce, but by the point in his life, Doc was not looking for trouble and left Joyce alone.

In May 1887, Holliday took a train to Glenwood Springs, Colorado. Glenwood Springs not only had gambling halls, it had waters that he hoped would help him the way the springs of New Mexico had. Unfortunately, they did not, and Doc's health deteriorated rapidly. In September, he developed pneumonia, from which he never recovered.

Naturally, Holliday's death has been the subject of controversy and speculation. On the morning of November 8, 1887, John Henry Holliday died at the Glenwood Hotel at the age of 36. Legend had it that as he lay dying, Holliday looked at his feet, presumably amused that he was dying with his boots off. For one of the West's most notorious gunslingers, Holliday and countless others probably assumed that he would "die with his boots on" in a gunfight. According to this legend, the nurses said that his last words were, "Damn, this is funny." Given his illness, however, modern historians believe Holliday would've been incapable of speaking coherently in his final days. It was also widely believed that Wyatt was there when Doc died, but Wyatt would not hear about his death for months. And even though Kate later claimed to have been there, most accounts say Holliday was alone when he died.

Given the course of Doc's life and death, perhaps it's not surprising that there is some speculation over his final resting place. It was believed that Doc was buried in Linwood Cemetery overlooking Glenwood Springs, but since it was November the frozen ground may have made it difficult for Holliday to actually be buried there, since it was was only accessible via a difficult mountain road. Holliday's biographer, Gary Roberts, has noted that other bodies were definitely transported to the Linwood Cemetery in November 1887, and that newspapers of the time stated Doc was buried there.

Even if Doc was buried there, the exact placement of his body was lost over time, leading the cemetery to erect a headstone in a random location on the grounds. However, the cemetery's initial headstone incorrectly listed the year of his birth as 1852 instead of 1851. Thus, it was eventually replaced by a more accurate headstone.

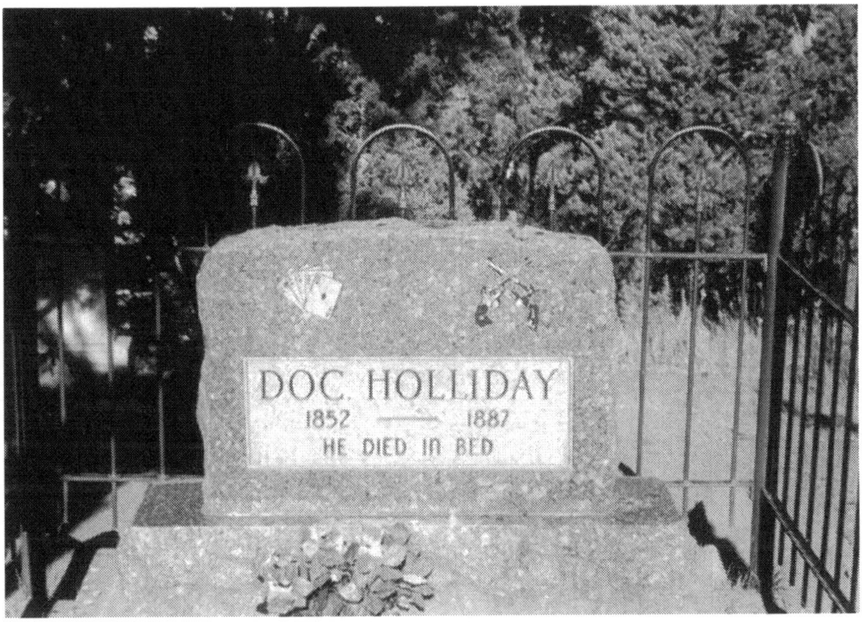
DOC. HOLLIDAY
1852 1887
HE DIED IN BED

Chapter 7: Wyatt and Sadie Roam the West

Like Nick and Virginia Earp before them, Wyatt and Sadie Earp roamed across the West after leaving Colorado and after spending a brief stint of time back in Dodge City. Spending time in locations as diverse as San Diego, San Francisco, Alaska, Nevada, and Los Angeles, Wyatt was always on the lookout for the path to riches, but he could never completely escape controversy or the events in Tombstone.

San Diego

San Diego in 1885 was rampant with gambling fever. Its mild climate was an attraction then, as it is now, and it drew in businessmen, investors, and others who had newly acquired wealth. For a man who was as entrenched in the gambling world as Earp, San Diego offered a lot of opportunity. He and Virgil managed as many as four saloons and gambling halls, the most famous of which was the Oyster Bar in what was then referred to as the Stingaree District, but is now the historic Gaslamp Quarter. Located in a Victorian house on 5th Avenue, gambling was not the only attraction at the Oyster Bar. The Golden Poppy was a brothel located on the upper floor and featured brightly painted rooms with women in dresses to match.

San Diego also nurtured another passion of Earp's: horse racing. He won his first horse, Otto Rex, in a poker game and ran the horse on the California harness racing circuit in the late 1890s. Wyatt and Sadie left San Diego to follow the circuit in 1890 but returned occasionally over the next decade to tend to property they owned. Earp's success in the gambling halls allowed him to dabble in the San Diego real estate market, and he owned at least 10 properties between 1888 and 1890. When the time came to list his occupation for the 1890 San Diego City Directory, Earp listed his as "capitalist."

The legal and illegal business interests in San Diego led to a booming crime rate and, at one point, San Diego had one of the worst crime rates in the country. Robbery, assault, and murder were not out of the ordinary, but Earp was in San Diego to make money, not fight crime. Still, Earp was connected enough to wield influence over the local police department. He was friends with the mayor, William Hunsaker, and he had an understanding with City Marshal Joseph Coyne that if the local police went into saloons, they were to look the other way when they saw gambling.

While Earp prospered in San Diego, his previous common-law wife, Mattie, had fallen on hard times. Mattie had left for California with Virgil and his wife when Wyatt left Tombstone for Colorado. She waited there for word from Wyatt regarding where and when she should meet him. When word never came, Mattie returned to Tombstone, which by this time was beyond its prime years. Even resorting to her previous trade as a prostitute was difficult because there were not enough men in town with the money to pay. She was found dead from an apparent suicide following a lethal combination of alcohol and laudanum on July 3, 1888. When the local coroner launched an inquest into her death, a Pinal County laborer, T.J. Flannery, said, "Earp, she said, had wrecked her life by deserting her and she didn't want to live."[6]

Ike Clanton managed to evade Wyatt Earp's vengeance, but he was on the wrong side of the barrel on June 1, 1887. Detective Jonas Brighton pursued Clanton and his brother, Phineas, on charges of cattle rustling and caught up with them in Springerville, Arizona. Phineas surrendered, but when Ike resisted arrest, Brighton shot and killed him.

San Francisco

The Earps also spent several years in San Francisco. Always a sportsman, Earp still enjoyed boxing, an interest developed in his days of working the Union Pacific railroad camps. He fed his love for the sport by refereeing and judging boxing matches. Many times Earp traveled across the San Diego border into Tijuana to referee matches, where money could be wagered out of the sight of the American authorities. These matches were not for the faint of heart. In one match in June 1888, the crowd grew so raucous that the Mexican policemen who were called in

---

[6] Bell, Bob Boze. *The Illustrated Life and Times of Wyatt Earp*. Page 97.

responded by pointing their revolvers at the mob to regain control.

When asked to referee a boxing match in San Francisco on December 2, 1896, Earp agreed. This was no undercover brawl in a backroom of Tijuana. This was a heavyweight prizefight with a purse of $10,000 between the famed Ruby Bob Fitzsimmons and the up-and-coming Tom Sharkey. The British Fitzsimmons made history by becoming boxing's first champion in three different weight divisions. Believing that James "Gentleman Jim" Corbett had retired and relinquished his crown, this fight was billed as the heavyweight championship of the world. Fitzsimmons was heavily favored, although rumors persisted that the fight was fixed to favor Sharkey. Initially unable to agree on a referee, the fighters eventually agreed on Earp.

Fitzsimmons

Boxing at the close of the 19th century was dogged by claims that it was too brutal. It had been outlawed in many towns, but as more rules were put in place to protect the fighters and instill some civility, boxing was experiencing something of a revival. Therefore, many in the crowd at Mechanics Pavilion were surprised to see Earp climb into the ring with a revolver strapped to his hip. Perhaps it was a habit from his experiences in Tijuana, but nonetheless, Earp had to be asked to surrender his firearm before the match could begin, for which he was fined $50.

When the fight commenced, it went as expected for the first seven rounds. Fitzsimmons was in control and seemingly on his way to victory. In the 8th round, Fitzsimmons unleashed a powerful punch to Sharkey's lower abdomen, sending Sharkey to the canvas. Earp called the punch a low blow and awarded the match to Sharkey, setting off pandemonium as Sharkey had to be carried from the ring. Fitzsimmons and his manager, who had heard the fix rumors, were incensed, as were those in the crowd who had their money on Fitzsimmons. Fitzsimmons sued for the purse in court, but the judge found no evidence that Earp was part of any fix and, saying that holding the match in the San Francisco city limits was illegal, anyway, allowed Sharkey to keep the winnings.

Despite the ruling, Earp was subject to a relentless torrent of accusatory articles and cartoons from the *San Francisco Call*. Every day for a month after the fight, the newspaper printed something about Earp, claiming that the fight was fixed and he was involved somehow. Earp denied it all, saying he called the fight as he saw it, but it did nothing to calm the furor that was regularly fed by the local writers. Later, it was revealed that at least one of the sportswriters lost money on the fight and was making Earp pay by crucifying him in print. Nonetheless, Earp was still seen in the boxing community. He was present for another Fitzsimmons fight, this time in a bout against the now un-retired Corbett in Carson City, Nevada in March 1897. Earp was not asked to referee, but he was asked to be a bouncer.

Eventually, though, as was the case in Tombstone, Earp found himself an enemy in his own community. Finally fed up with the fallout from the fight, Earp sold all of his sporting assets and turned his attention north.

Alaska, Seattle, and Back Again

Earp in Alaska

Wyatt and Sadie followed the rush to Alaska, where gold had been discovered in the Klondike and near Nome. In 1899, Earp and Charles E. Hoxie opened the Dexter Saloon, although this was not Earp's only business venture that year. He also had business interests in Seattle, Washington.

Like it was in many towns that were opening in the West, gambling was rampant in Seattle. Technically, gambling was illegal there, but the level of tolerance fluctuated, and it was not hard to find in the city's Tenderloin District. John Considine was the leader of the Seattle gambling scene, and when Earp came into town in November 1899 with the intention of opening a gambling hall, Considine was not pleased. The people of Seattle were not sure what to think, either. Both the *Seattle Daily Times* and the *Seattle Post Intelligencer* made reference to Earp's debacle in the Fitzsimmons versus Sharkey match, although they could not agree on whether he was an evil troublemaker or an asset to the community.

After learning of Earp's business plans, a group of Considine's men paid Earp and his partner, local businessman Thomas Urquhart, a visit and suggested that they take their business outside of Seattle. If Earp could not agree to that, they told him to check in with the police chief, C.S. Reed, whom they assumed would not be happy to have Earp in town. Earp told Considine's crew in no uncertain terms that he was going to open his saloon and he was not going to line Reed's pocket with payoff money because he assumed Considine was paying him enough for the both of them.

Earp and Urquhart proceeded with their plans and opened the Union Club on Second Avenue. The politics of Seattle impacted whether or not gambling was legal or simply tolerated at any given time. When gambling was reinstated with a set of strict rules – which were broken enough that the city was collecting a windfall in fines – the Union Club was a good moneymaker for its owners. Urquhart was able to buy out Earp and he became the sole proprietor of the Union Club when Earp's brief stay in Seattle ended in 1900.

Alaska and Nevada

Nome, Alaska was yet another western boomtown when Wyatt and Sadie lived there in 1900. Parts of town were literally lined with tents, as gold prospectors were simply looking for a place to sleep before heading back out to look for gold. As was the case with other boomtowns, gambling, drinking, and prostitution were not hard to find. In an environment like this, it was also not difficult for Wyatt to end up in skirmishes with the law. On June 29, after he had been back in town for just about a month, Earp was arrested for interfering with an officer who was attempting to break up a street brawl. A few months later, Wyatt and Sadie's brother, Nathan, were arrested in the Dexter Saloon after being charged with beating an Army officer who tried to arrest a bar patron for disorderly conduct.

While Earp was in Alaska, his younger brother, Warren, was shot and killed in a barfight in Willcox, Arizona. The youngest of the Earp brothers, Warren worked as a bartender and a stagecoach driver. He was also notorious for being an angry drunk, frequently finding himself in trouble for his temper. Cochise County authorities declined to prosecute the shooter, ranch foreman Henry Hooker. Rumors that Earp left Alaska to seek vengeance for his brother's death were false.

Meanwhile, despite the fact that Earp had moved on, the San Francisco media continued to dredge up the controversy surrounding the Fitzsimmons/Sharkey match. In September 1900, a San Francisco sportswriter wrote a story about the history of the Earp family. The story was packed with lies, including the number of men Earp killed. Having grown tired of what he viewed as lies and misrepresentations of events, Earp began to think about writing his memoirs. His attempt to get his version of his life story in print would continue for the rest of his life.

On December 12, 1901, the *Los Angeles Times* reported the arrival of Wyatt and Sadie in Southern California after their stay in Alaska. While Wyatt claimed that his business interests in Nome were doing well financially, the fact that he never returned to Nome suggests otherwise. The Earps did find their way to Tonopah, Nevada, though. In 1902, Wyatt drove into town with a wagon full of bar fixtures and he opened the Northern Saloon. A friend managed the bar while Earp went off prospecting, but his stay in Nevada was not fruitful. After briefly holding a job as deputy to Marshal J.F. Emmit, Wyatt and Sadie made their way back to Los Angeles in 1903. They would spend their remaining years traveling back and forth between Southern California and Parker, Arizona, near the Colorado River. They had a mining claim there that never paid off, but Earp felt most at home when he was in the desert and, fittingly, he named the mine "Happy Days."

Wyatt's saloon in Tonopah, Nevada in 1902. It's very likely that his wife, Josie, is on the horse on the left.

South of Tonopah, in 1904, Virgil Earp worked as a bouncer for a saloon in the small town of Goldfield, which was thriving after the discovery of gold in 1902. In January 1905, Virgil was appointed deputy sheriff of Esmeralda County. Wyatt and Sadie joined Virgil and his wife there and put in some mining claims, but their stay was brief. Virgil contracted pneumonia and died on October 18, 1905. Soon after Virgil's death, his wife went to live near Virgil's family and Wyatt and Sadie returned to Los Angeles.

Los Angeles

Old frontiersmen started drifting into Los Angeles in the early 1900s. Many of the boomtowns were on their way to becoming ghost towns and a new industry - movies - offered opportunities for men used to real-life brawling to work as stuntmen. Some were even offered small roles on camera as extras. There was no need to worry about speaking lines; "talkies" did not begin until Al Jolson appeared in "The Jazz Singer" in 1927.

Wyatt Earp never appeared in a movie, but he did love watching them. Exactly how he earned a living during his years in Los Angeles is something of a mystery. It would not be unexpected for a former lawman and gambler to fall back on those skills whenever necessary. In October 1910, he was asked by the Los Angeles Police Department commissioner to ride out into San Bernardino County to remove those with illegal mining claims. A friend of the Earp family claimed that he served as Wyatt's deputy on special missions for the Los Angeles Police Department. Arthur King reported that he and Earp traveled into Mexico to track down fugitives of the law. Once located, King reported he and Earp brought the fugitives back to Los Angeles to stand trial, which was a quicker process than waiting up to two years for the Mexican government to extradite those who were wanted by the law.

Unfortunately for Wyatt, times were changing, and gambling was not as accepted as it had been in his heyday in Tombstone or even Nome. In July 1911, Earp was arrested for his role in an illegal game of faro, a favorite card game on the frontier, at a Los Angeles hotel. Wyatt was implicated as the organizer of the game, though he claimed he was merely a participant. Incensed at what he perceived as yet another assault on his character, he told his side of the story to the *Los Angeles Examiner*, and called on Henry Gage, the former governor of California, to serve as a character witness. The charges were eventually dropped due to a lack of evidence and this marked the last time that Wyatt, now in his 60s, would read his name in the paper as the result of skirmishes with the law.

Hollywood

The fact that movie sets were open during the silent movie era made it easy for the curious to wander around the movie lot and watch the filming. Earp was no exception. John Ford, who went on to become a legendary film director, once served Earp coffee on a movie set, and Earp counted Tom Mix, one of the first stars of Western films, as one of his friends. He also became acquainted with a young Marion Morrison and years later, after Morrison had taken the name John Wayne, he said he modeled his portrayal of western lawmen on Earp.

The Duke

When Earp was in Alaska, he also met author Jack London. The writer set two of his most famous novels, "White Fang" and "The Call of the Wild" in the Klondike Gold Rush. One day when London was in Los Angeles, he and Earp decided to track down former cowboy turned movie director, Raoul Walsh. They wanted to meet the man who had convinced Mexican revolutionary Pancho Villa to star in the 1914 biographic film, "The Life of General Villa."

As Walsh was taking a break at the movie studio, an assistant told him that two men were there to see him, one going by the name London. After confirming that the man named London had the first name Jack, Walsh told the assistant to send them in. The trio went to dinner at Al Levy's Café, owned by one of early Los Angeles' leading restaurateurs, Al Levy. The specialty of the house was a new sensation, oyster cocktails. While the men ate, one of the world's most famous entertainers, Charlie Chaplin, approached their table. When Walsh introduced his dinner guests to the movie star, Chaplin said to Earp, "You're the bloke from Arizona, aren't you? Tamed the baddies, huh?"[7]

Earp's best friend in Hollywood was William S. Hart, an actor, director, producer, and screenwriter. Hart portrayed men of the Western frontier before Tom Mix did, and their styles were very different. Hart's characters were dark and gritty, while Mix brought much more flair and flash to the screen. Earp told of his attempts to teach Hart the art of the "quick draw," but Hart dropped his gun so often during the transfer out of his holster that they had to put a towel on the floor to keep it from being damaged.

---

[7] Barra, Allen. "Wyatt on the Set!" *True West Magazine,* May 7, 2012.

The Quest to Set the Record Straight

As late as 1922, Earp was still the subject of scathing newspaper articles. *Los Angeles Times* reporter J.M. Scanland's story about Earp's days as a lawman, titled "Lurid Trails are Left by Olden Day Bandits," had at least one glaring error: it said that Earp was dead. Sadie was furious at the slanted article and contacted the *Times* to tell them so. Earp took it a step further two years later and went to the reporter's home to confront him, resulting in an effusive verbal and written apology.

Still, Earp wanted to more fully clear his name. John Flood and Earp met in 1905 and Flood, an engineer, became Earp's personal secretary. Flood made an attempt at writing the biography, but he was an engineer, not a writer. His manuscript was simply not well written. Sadie and Wyatt asked Hart to use his connections to help get the book published, but even a Hollywood heavyweight like Hart had no luck. Rejection letters came in with every attempt at publication, starting with a query to the *Saturday Evening Post* to see if the magazine was interested in serializing Earp's story. The feedback Earp and Hart received criticized both the content and the style of the manuscript. One publisher simply said that the story was not interesting.

Hart and Earp were discussing possibilities for suitable collaborators that might improve on Flood's manuscript when, in late 1928, Earp was approached by a writer from San Diego, Stuart Lake. Lake had served as press secretary during the presidency of Teddy Roosevelt, one of the nation's great outdoorsman and a lover of the West. Roosevelt had a conversation with Bat Masterson, one of the Wild West's most famous characters and a friend of Earp's. Masterson, among other things, was a former lawman, and, like Earp, an avid gambler and former deputy in Dodge City. Unlike Earp, though, Masterson left the West and started a career as a sportswriter in New York City around 1883. He never forgot about Earp, though, and told Roosevelt, with Lake listening, that it was Earp that really epitomized what the West was all about.

When Masterson died while typing his column for the *New York Telegraph* in 1921, Lake determined that if he was going to contact Earp and write his story, he needed to start trying to locate him before it was too late. When Earp finally heard from him, he liked Lake and his credentials. He told Hart in a letter that they had enjoyed his conversations with Lake and suggested that perhaps Lake would be the one to finally help him get his memoirs published. Even as Earp's health was declining, he was concerned with the accuracy of his life story in print.

The Earps lived far from the lap of luxury in Wyatt's final years. When not at their mining camp near Parker, they rented small, inexpensive bungalows close to downtown Los Angeles. Sadie's sister sent money regularly, but there were reports that she used that money to sustain her own gambling habit. Often, the Earps relied on the generosity of Charles Welsh and his family, friends from the Alaska days, who offered the Earps a place to stay.

On January 7, 1929, Earp wrote a letter to Hart and told him that his brother, Newton, had died at the age of 91 shortly before Christmas. Those close to the Earps knew that the end was near for Wyatt, too. Wyatt Earp died in his Los Angeles home on January 13, 1929 at the age of 80. It is reported that his last words were, "Suppose. Suppose."

Chapter 8: Wyatt Dies but a Star is Born

Wyatt Earp in later years, 1925

In a fitting tribute to the former lawman and true icon of the West, Tom Mix and William Hart, who portrayed lives on screen that Earp actually lived, served as pallbearers at Earp's funeral. Sadie was too distraught to attend. Earp's body was cremated and the remains were sent to Colma, California, where his gravesite attracts regular visitors.

While Wyatt Earp had developed a reputation – and not always a positive one – and many in the West knew of him, he was not actually famous when he died, let alone the household name that he is today. Even among those who knew who he was, it is not likely that anyone other than Sadie really knew Wyatt, other than tales about the 30 second gunfight in Tombstone, which itself had been largely forgotten decades earlier. Earp himself was partially responsible for this. It is accepted by a consensus of historians that both Sadie and Wyatt told versions of the truth, rather than the complete truth, about Earp's life.

After Earp's death, Stuart Lake moved forward with Earp's biography. Sadie fought to have the publication stopped, wanting to both protect Wyatt's reputation and avoid any mention of herself in the book. Lake assured her that he would protect Earp's legacy, and he kept his promise with a flattering, semi-fictional account of Earp's life in *Wyatt Earp: Frontier Marshal*. Published in 1931, his biography was not the first one to offer a sensationalized account of Earp's life. Walter Burns called Earp "The Lion of Tombstone" in his 1927 book, *Tombstone, An Iliad of the Southwest*, a publication that Earp feared would interfere with his attempts to get his own book in print. Years later, Lake, admitted to fabricating several of the quotes he attributed to Earp. However, it is important to keep the book in context. It was written during the Great Depression, and Americans were searching for escape and heroes more than harsh reality. Lake was also not a trained historian and did not set out to write a scholarly text.

Despite the inaccuracies, *Wyatt Earp: Frontier Marshal* set the wheels in motion for the birth of the legendary, even if inaccurate, Wyatt Earp. A glimpse of this was seen shortly before Earp died. The 1928 movie "In Old Arizona" was the first western talkie and featured Warner Baxter as Sergeant Mickey Dunn, charged with finding the robber of a Tombstone stagecoach. Raoul Welsh directed the film and the character of Dunn drew from Earp's life. It also marked the introduction of the singing cowboy, which became a popular movie attraction.

This was followed by numerous characters in books, movies, and television that were either loosely or closely based on Earp. As would be expected, the Gunfight at the O.K. Corral made great movie fodder, starting with 1932's "Law and Order." The film gave an account of the Gunfight at the O.K. Corral and was based on the novel "Saint Johnson," written by W.R. Burnett. The Earp character is named Frame Johnson and was first played by John Huston. In the remake in 1953, the future president, Ronald Reagan, portrayed Johnson. In 1934, Lake's book was made into the movie, "Frontier Marshal," this time with the name Michael Earp in place of Wyatt. The name Wyatt Earp was finally used in film in 1942 in 'Tombstone," featuring another retelling of the gunfight in Tombstone. Acting legend Henry Fonda played Wyatt in the 1953 film, "My Darling Clementine."

Earp made it to television in 1955, when westerns were all the rage. Hugh O'Brien played him in the ABC series, "The Life and Legend of Wyatt Earp," which aired until 1961. Joel McRae took his turn at playing Wyatt in the movie "Wichita" in 1955 and in 1957, one of the more acclaimed efforts involving Earp's legend, "Gunfight at the O.K. Corral" was released, starring Burt Lancaster as Wyatt. The film was nominated for two Academy Awards.

In 1971, Earp returned to the movies in "Hour of the Gun," starring James Garner. It was another 20 years before Earp would return to the silver screen, this time in the 1993 movie "Tombstone." Kurt Russell stars as Earp, and for the first time, his relationship with Sadie was explored in film with Dana Delaney playing Earp's third wife. A year later, Kevin Costner starred in "Wyatt Earp," which explored his life from his teen years through his prospecting days in Alaska.

Earp's image can be found in more than just movies. The U.S. Postal Service featured him on a postage stamp in 1994 as part of its Legends of the West Series. His name and likeness have been used to sell cap guns, clothing, pocket watches, and action figures. Fans of the West can easily find replica guns, hats, badges, and holsters. The small town of Tombstone continues to capitalize on Earp and the legendary gunfight that haunted him, offering a reenactment of the battle every afternoon.

Sadie Earp died in 1944. Glenn Boyer published what were originally believed to be her memoirs in "I Married Wyatt Earp" in 1976. However, after it was discovered that much of the book was fabricated, the University of Arizona Press removed it from its catalog, and historians no longer consider it a historically accurate document.

Long after his death, Wyatt Earp continues to be portrayed as a hero of the West, despite the fact that there it little evidence to suggest that he was one in any traditional interpretation of the word. He was a flawed man living in a time and place where society's rules and the nation's laws were not what they are today. The fact that Earp has been held up as symbol of the heroism of the West, over a century after he walked the streets of Tombstone, is largely the work of America's need for heroes, as well as the nation's desire to interpret its history through a glossier, more adventurous prism. Perhaps it is all the more fitting that Earp has become the most famous man of the Wild West, which itself continues to be widely celebrated for its lawlessness and viewed as uniquely American. .

Even if Earp was not a hero, there is no doubt that Earp was a survivor who lived a life that spanned an incredible series of events in America's history. A young boy during the Civil War and an elderly man just as the country was about to fall into the Great Depression, Earp saw an enormous amount of change in his country. Even for those who do not view Earp as a hero, he remains a symbol of the West and a link to the nation's past.

Chapter 9: The Doc Holliday Legend

Like other men of the Western frontier, especially his friend Wyatt Earp, Doc Holliday was as much myth as man after his death. At least part of his story has been depicted in film, including "My Darling Clementine" in 1936, "Gunfight at the OK Corral" in 1957, and "Tombstone" in 1993. Stacy Keach played him in the first movie to feature him as the main character in "Doc" in 1971. In 2011, Mary Doria Russell published the critically acclaimed novel, "Doc," a work of historical fiction that has been hailed by critics for shining new light on the man that everyone thought they already knew. Later that year, HBO announced that Doc would be getting his own television series, based on Russell's novel.

Doc Holliday did not lead the life that seemed to be his destiny. John Henry Holliday was an educated, handsome, and witty man could have been a dentist and a member of high society in the South. Instead, circumstances both within his control and outside of his control conspired to create Doc Holliday, who spent his adult life under the dark image of a cold-blooded killer in the West, a reputation that was unquestionably partly his own creation. In one interview with a newspaper, after being asked if his conscience ever troubled him, Holliday reportedly answered, "I coughed that up with my lungs years ago."

Holliday left behind no documents, no records, and no children to tell his story, leaving historians to piece together the life of a boy who grew up during the Reconstruction Era in the South and became an icon of the West. This has left much open to interpretation, making an accurate profile of his life extremely challenging. Virgil Earp himself may have summed it up best in an 1882 interview with the Arizona Daily Star, explaining, "There was something very peculiar about Doc. He was gentlemanly, a good dentist, a friendly man, and yet outside of us boys I don't think he had a friend in the Territory. Tales were told that he had murdered men in different parts of the country; that he had robbed and committed all manner of crimes, and yet when persons were asked how they knew it, they could only admit that it was hearsay, and that nothing of the kind could really be traced up to Doc's account."

Regardless of which Holliday stories are true or embellished legend, what is clear is that Holliday had no great achievements that might set him apart from other men of the 19th century. And yet he has become a household name, second perhaps only to Wyatt Earp among the legends of the West. Why is there so much interest in a man that many believe was a hotheaded gunman at best and a killer at worst, even if neither are completely accurate descriptions him? Perhaps it is in the empathy for the boy that lost his mother to the same dreaded disease that would kill him. Perhaps it is a measure of understanding for a man who could not have his one true love because she happened to be his cousin. Perhaps it is simply because the idea of a dentist running with the likes of Wyatt Earp is too good of a story to pass up. Whatever the reasons, Holliday the man will certainly continue to be obscured by Holliday the legend, which has made him an indelible figure of the West.

Wyatt Earp Bibliography

Barra, Allen. *Inventing Wyatt Earp: His Life and Many Legends.* New York: Carroll & Graf Publishers. 1998

Barra, Allen. "Wyatt on the Set!" *True West Magazine.* May 7, 2012.

Bell, Bob Boze. *The Illustrated Life and Times of Wyatt Earp.* Phoenix: Tri-Star Boze Publications, 1995.

Gatto, Steve. *The Real Wyatt Earp.* Silver City, New Mexico: High Lonesome Books, 2000.

Tefertiller, Casey. *Wyatt Earp: The Life Behind the Legend.* New York: Wiley and Sons, 1997.

Turner, Alfred, ed. *The O.K. Corral Inquest.* College Station, Texas: Creative Publishing Company, 1981.

Doc Holliday Bibliography

"Bat Masterson Not Impressed by Doc Holliday." *Territorial News.* December 15, 2010.

Bell, Bob Boze. *The Illustrated Life and Times of Doc Holliday.* Phoenix: Tri-Star Boze Publications, 1994.

Guinn, Jeff. *The Last Gunfight.* New York: Simon & Schuster. 2011.

Roberts, Gary L. *Doc Holliday: The Life and Legend.* Hoboken, New Jersey: Wiley & Sons. 2006.

Turner, Alfred, ed. *The O.K. Corral Inquest.* College Station, Texas: Creative Publishing Company, 1981.

Printed in Great Britain
by Amazon.co.uk, Ltd.,
Marston Gate.